GRACE

Copyright © 2022 Grace Larson
All right reserved

No part of this book may be reproduced, or stored in retrieval system, or transmitted in any form of by any means, electronics, mechanical, photocopying, recording, or otherwise, without express written permission of the author.

Cover design by: US BOOK PRESS Printed in the United States of America

GRACE

Written by

Anne Gold

Based on the book of the same name
by **Grace Larson**

EXT. SHEEP RANCH - DAY

SUPER: 1944

The CAMERA is high above an idyllic ranch. Sheep graze on the polished meadow. Morning birds chirp, flying into an azure sky. A twostory, white house stands in middle of the ranch.

INT. KITCHEN - DAY

JANE (50s) cooks fried eggs on a wood stove which has a reservoir. A couple of Sad Irons sit on the counter on the side.

INT. KITCHEN - LATER

Jane sets plates on a table covered with a bright yellow oil cloth. SANDY (early 20s), a beautiful, poised young lady enters.

      SANDY
    Let me help you, Mom.

Sandy rolls up her sleeves and places perfectly cooked eggs onto the plates. Jane glances at her daughter.

      JANE
   You've got paint on you again.

Sandy looks down at a stroke of red paint on her forearm and shrugs.

      SANDY
    It will wash off.

RAY (late 20s), tousle-haired, slides into the room.
      RAY
    Good morning.

> JANE
> (to Ray)
> Breakfast is almost ready.

Jane hands Sandy a basket of bread.

> SANDY
> Where's Dad?

> JANE
> Probably still in bed. And where's
> Grace

> RAY
> Probably in the Carlin House.

> SANDY
> (to Ray) Shall we?

> RAY
> Yep.

Sandy yells into upstairs as Ray exits through the back door.

> SANDY
> Dad!

> RAY (O.S.)
> Grace!

EXT. SHEEP RANCH - DAY

About 50 feet away from the house next to a wood shed is an out house.

INT. THE CARLIN HOUSE - DAY

The place is strewn with all kinds of stuff: Lincoln logs, old toys, books and magazines. Ray opens the door and pokes his head in.

                    RAY
                    Grace?

A cherubic face appears behind a book. GRACE (5), ensconced in a corner among countless books, looks up with bright eyes.

                    GRACE
                    Hi, Uncle Ray!

                    RAY
                    Time for brekkie.

                    GRACE
                    Yay!

                    RAY
                    Hungry?

                    GRACE
                    Famished!

Ray laughs.
                    RAY
                    Where did you learn that word?

INT. KITCHEN – DAY

GRANDPA CARL (50s) sits over a cup of coffee at the table, surveying a newspaper article. Grace and Ray walk in.
                    GRACE
            Good morning, Grandpa Carl! Good morning,
               Grandma Jane! Good morning, Aunt Sandy!

Sandy sweeps Grace into a hug.

                    SANDY

>   Morning, Angel.

Grace sits down and swallows an entire fried egg whole.

>   GRACE
>   (to Jane)
>   No one cooks eggs as well as you,
>   Grandma Jane.

>   Jane
>   looks at Grace lovingly.

>   JANE
>   You can have as much as you want,
>   my darling.

>   GRACE
>   Am I getting maple milk today?

>   JANE
>   Oh, that's right.

Jane takes out a canned milk from a bowl of water that has a stalk of celery in it.

>   GRACE
>   Why do you put the celery in there?

>   JANE

We keep the celery cool so it can keep the milk cool We don't have a refrigerator.

>   GRACE
>   How strange.

The adults erupt in laughter.

EXT. SHEEP RANCH - AFTERNOON

A huge black walnut tree stands near the wood shed. Grace sits on the ground that's covered with fallen walnuts, trying to crack those tough shelled nuts.

INT. SITTING ROOM/JANE AND CARL'S HOUSE - NIGHT

Wooden floors; a small wood heater in the middle of the room; a round oak table in one corner.
Carl, under the illumination of a dim light bulb, riffles through an issue of National Geographic. Jane sweeps the floor, sporadically sprinkling coffee grounds to keep the dust down.

Carl folds the corner of a page.

>   CARL
>   Yellowstone National Park. Remind
>   me to let Grace have a look at it.

Jane smiles.

>   JANE
>   She would love to ride horses there,
>   wouldn't she?

INT. BEDROOM/JANE AND CARL'S HOUSE - NIGHT

In a twin bed, Grace is sunk in sleep.

EXT. JANE AND CARL'S HOUSE - MORNING

Grace, in high spirits, dances out of the house. She flings her arms over her head and stretches. Right by the door, a very large, yellow rose bush blooms. Grace gulps a great lungful of its aroma and lets out a satisfied sigh.

INT. THE CARLIN HOUSE - DAY

Grace pores over a book when she hears people talking to each other loudly.
Curious, Grace abandons her read.

EXT. SHEEP RANCH - DAY

Grace discovers that several HERDERS are moving the sheep. She sees Ray, on a pack horse that carries a tent, going after the herders.

GRACE
Uncle Ray! What are you doing?

Ray looks over his shoulder.

RAY
Getting the camps ready, Grace!
We're moving the sheep out to pasture!

INT. KITCHEN - DAY

Sandy and Jane gather stoves and kitchen supplies when Grace dashes in.

GRACE
Can I help, Grandma Jane?

Jane and Sandy look at Grace, then at each other.

GRACE (CONT'D)
Oh, please do let me help. Please!

EXT. JANE AND CARL'S HOUSE - DAY

Sandy helps Grace onto a horse. Grace looks comfortable; she's ridden numerous times.

SANDY
You see where Uncle Ray is?

Grace nods.

                    SANDY (CONT'D)
                Good. Just go and give these to him.

Sandy stows a bag on the horse.

                    SANDY (CONT'D)
                He will know what to do next, okay?

                         GRACE
                      Yes, Aunt Sandy.

Grace sets off.

INT. SANDY'S ROOM - LATER

Sandy is painting when she hears an awful lot of clanging. She puts down her brush and dashes to the window.

Jaw-dropped, Sandy sees a pack horse racing along the fence dragging a camp stove. On its back is a desperate Grace who's too small to get off the big saddle. Behind them, frying pans, tin plates, and coffee pots scatter along the trail.

INT. JANE AND CARL'S HOUSE - DAY

Sandy runs down the stairs two at a time.

EXT. SHEEP RANCH - DAY

Sandy zooms to the gate where the pack horse is coming through. She successfully stops the animal, saving Grace.

                         GRACE
                     (panting heavily)
                    I dropped everything.
Sandy takes Grace off the saddle.

                         SANDY

Are you okay?!

GRACE
I'm okay, Aunt Sandy.

SANDY
Thank god!

GRACE
But....

SANDY
But what?

GRACE
I think the stove is beyond repair....

INT. SITTING ROOM/JANE AND CARL'S HOUSE - NIGHT

Jane is on the phone.

JANE
She's fine.
(beat)
Tomorrow? Okay.... What time will you be here?
(beat)
Nine in the morning? So, we will expect you around noon.
(MORE)

JANE (CONT'D)
(beat)
Don't snap at me. You're never on time.

On the stairs, Grace listens to the conversation, looking dismal.

INT. BEDROOM/JANE AND CARL'S HOUSE - DAY

Grace looks around the room dolefully.

SANDY (O.S.)

                    Grace?

Without replying, Grace grabs a small bag from her bed. Sandy walks in.
                SANDY (CONT'D)
            Your mom is here.
Grace nods, trying not to betray her desire to cry. Sandy pulls her into an embrace.

                SANDY (CONT'D)
        I know, Angel. We will miss you too.

INT. CAR - MOVING - DAY

Grace is in the passenger seat. Grace's mom, HAZEL (20s), a woman who looks like she's seen better days, drives. PATTY (3), Grace's little sister, sits in the back.

                    HAZEL
                  (to Grace)
        I knew you would cause some sort of trouble.

Grace looks outside the window, not muttering a word.

INT. KITCHEN/HAZEL'S HOUSE - NIGHT

Hazel, Patty, Grace and her dad, HAROLD (30s), eat dinner in silence. Grace stares down at a dry-looking moose steak on her plate.
                    GRACE
                  (to Hazel)
        Can I go to bed, Mom? I'm tired.

Hazel looks at Grace's food, brows raised.

                    HAZEL
        You know you are expected to eat everything.

                    GRACE
It's cold and I don't like how the tallow feels in my mouth.

                    HAZEL
Finish your food now or you don't get dinner tomorrow.

                    GRACE
                    But --

                    HAZEL
I don't want to hear another word from you!

Grace cuts a piece of the meat and puts it in her mouth, struggling to swallow it.

EXT. HAZEL'S HOUSE - DAY

A carpet of golden leaves on the ground. Patty stamps on them, giggling at the crunching sound under her feet.

INT. LIVING ROOM/HAZEL'S HOME - DAY

On a threadbare sofa, Harold listens to the radio with intense concentration. Grace sits on the floor, absorbed in a book.

                    MAN
                (on the radio)
World News Today by CBS. We are here to bring you first-hand news from political and battle crimes in America and many foreign lands. Now, here is Douglas Edward....

EXT. HAZEL'S HOME - DAY

Patty attempts at a run but drops on all fours. She lets out an ear-splitting cry.

          INT. LIVING ROOM/HAZEL'S HOME - DAY

15

Harold turns sharply to Grace.
HAROLD

What are you doing here?! Why aren't you watching your sister?!

Hazel hurries into the room.

HAZEL
(to Harold)
What's the matter?

HAROLD
She let Patty play outside on her own!

Hazel walks straight to Grace and pulls her hair back violently. Grace yelps.

HAZEL
I told you to keep an eye on your sister!

GRACE
I'm sorry, Mom!

Hazel gives Grace another hard pull before releasing her grip.

HAZEL
Useless!

Hazel hastens outside.

EXT. HAZEL'S HOME – DAY

Hazel picks up a sobbing Patty.

INT. LIVING ROOM/HAZEL'S HOME - DAY

Harold shakes his head, annoyed, and turns up the volume of his radio. Grace rubs her head, fighting back her tears.

EXT. BARN - DAY
Grace pushes a barrow of hay into the barn with Patty at her elbow.

INT. BARN - DAY

Grace cleans the stalls.

EXT. BARN - DAY

A few horses nibble on the grass. Patty looks at them, intrigued.

INT. BARN - DAY

Patty runs to her sister.
　　　　　　　　　　PATTY
　　　　　　　　　Horse!

Grace looks at Patty, puzzled.

　　　　　　　　PATTY (CONT'D)
　　　　　　　Horse! Go up!

　　　　　　　　　　GRACE
　　　　　　You wanna get on one?

Patty nods vehemently.

EXT. BARN – DAY

Grace places a stool next to a horse and steps on it. She holds Patty up and mounts her onto the horse. Patty laughs, thrilled with excitement.
　　　　　　　　　　GRACE
　　　　　　　　　Stay on.

INT. BARN - LATER

Grace adds hay into a stall when she hears a thud.

EXT. BARN – DAY

Grace runs out of the barn and gasps as she sees Patty lying motionless on the ground and completely knocked out.

INT. KITCHEN/HAZEL'S HOME - DAY

Grace sprints into the kitchen to Hazel.

                GRACE
                Mom!

                HAZEL
                What is it?

                GRACE
                I killed her.

                HAZEL
                What?!

                GRACE
                Patty. I killed her.

Hazel looks at Grace, aghast.

EXT. BARN - DAY

Hazel sinks to the ground next to Patty.

                HAZEL
                Patty?

Hazel shakes her girl's shoulders frantically. Grace hovers nervously behind them.

                HAZEL (CONT'D)
                Patty!

Miraculously, Patty's eyelashes flutter and she opens her eyes. Hazel lets out a cry of relief.

EXT. HAZEL'S HOME - DAY

Grace is leaned over a wood chopping block. Hazel whacks her with a stick of wood, looking mad in her rage. Grace shuts her eyes in pain and tears seep from behind her lids.

EXT. HAZEL'S HOME - DAY

Winter is everywhere; thick snow glistens under the sun; Trees bare and bleak.

INT. KITCHEN/HAZEL'S HOUSE - DAY

Grace walks into the kitchen when Hazel is washing a cream separator.

> GRACE
> Mom, can I go play on the
> Sled Uncle Ray gave me?

Hazel shoots Grace a sharp look.

> HAZEL
> Play? No time for that.
> Go and get me the milk.

EXT. HAZEL'S HOME - DAY

Grace trudges through snow, carrying two buckets of milk. She suddenly falls on the ice and spills both buckets. Grace looks down at her pants which are soaked in milk.

EXT. HAZEL'S HOME - DAY

Wet pants pulled down to her ankles, Grace gets another spanking.
EXT. CHERRY ORCHARD - DAY

Hazel and Harold pasture horses and the girls play on the side. A FARMER (30s) leers at Patty as he drives by in a pickup.

INT. RESTROOM/CHERRY ORCHARD - DAY
Grace walks in and bolts the door.
EXT. CHERRY ORCHARD - DAY
Grace comes back to find her sister but doesn't see Patty anywhere.
EXT. CHERRY ORCHARD - LATER
Grace looks around.

                    GRACE
                    Patty?

Grace spots the farmer's pickup parked outside a shed.

EXT. SHED – DAY
Grace sneaks over to the shed and is openmouthed when she sees the farmer strip down his pants in front of a bemused Patty.

                    FARMER
         Wanna know how sex works, little girl?

Grace scampers away.

EXT. SHEEP RANCH - DAY

Another glorious summer. Grace (7) flies into Sandy's arms. Behind them, Patty (5) eyes the two dispassionately.

INT. SITTING ROOM/JANE AND CARL'S HOUSE - DAY

Sandy hands a cat to Grace. Grace wows in surprised delight.

SANDY Isn't he cute?

Grace strokes the cat gently. Patty looks at the pet with distaste.

EXT. SHEEP RANCH - DAY

Patty takes Grace by the hand and leads her to the back of the house, Grace's cat prancing at their heels.

GRACE
What is it that you want to show me?

PATTY
Shh! Something fun.

They stop at a big 500 gallon stock tank. Grace looks at it, stony-faced.

GRACE
This is your idea of fun?
Patty smiles, something dark lurking behind her lifted lips.

PATTY
No, but this is.

Patty scoops the cat up into her arms and dunks the animal under water. Grace screams.

GRACE
What are you doing?! Stop!

The cat cries in misery. Grace stomps her feet, tears sliding down her face.

GRACE (CONT'D)
Stop!!!
Patty, still wearing that dark smile,
lets the cat go.

INT. THE CARLIN HOUSE - AFTERNOON

Jane opens the door of the Carlin House and is surprised to find Grace.

                    JANE
        Grace! Everyone was wondering where
                   you went.

Grace raises her head, her eyes red and swollen. Jane walks in at
                           once.

                 JANE (CONT'D)

          Oh, Sweetie. What's the matter?

                    GRACE
                   I hate her.

                  JANE Who?

                    GRACE
                    Patty.

Jane is flabbergasted.
                    JANE
        She's your sister. What makes you say that?

Grace shakes her head in despair.

                    GRACE
   I know I'm wicked, Grandma Jane. But I resent her so much!

Jane pauses momentarily, arranging her thoughts.

                    JANE
         Come, Grace. There's something
               I want to show you.

        INT. SITTING ROOM/JANE AND CARL'S HOUSE -
                      AFTERNOON

                          22

Jane sits Grace down and takes out a photo album. Jane shows Grace a photo of her mother in a simple wedding dress and a man whom Grace does not recognize. Grace looks at the black-and-white picture in bewilderment.

> JANE
> That's your dad.

Grace looks unblinkingly at her grandma.

> GRACE
> He's not.

> JANE
> Harold is Patty's dad, not yours. Your father is this man. He left when you were a baby. I always think... maybe this is why you and Patty are so different....

Jane sighs and pats Grace consolingly on the shoulder. Grace stares blankly at the face of her real father.

EXT. BIG ARM SCHOOL - DAY

SUPER: 1948

A wood-fame building with an American flag flying on top of a sliver flagpole at the front.

INT. CLASSROOM - DAY

Grace (9) studies an arithmetic workbook when a BOY passes her.
> BOY
> Horse face.

Grace colors up instantly. The boy sits down next to some other BOYS who are all sniggering.

> BOY (CONT'D)

                    (to his friends)
               And what's that on her legs?

Grace instinctively covers her leg which is suffering from painful-looking boils with her hands.

                    BOY (CONT'D)
               Gross!

The boys howl with laughter which soon evaporates when their teacher, MRS. LANNAN, a spectacled woman, walks into the room.

                    MRS. LANNAN
               Quiet down, everyone.
               Let's begin today's lesson.

INT. CLASSROOM - LATER
Mid-class.

                    MRS. LANNAN
               Who can spell "Ballerina"?

A GIRL shoots her hand in the air.

                    MRS. LANNAN (CONT'D)
               Leanne.

Leanne stands up.
                    LEANNE
               B-a-l-l-e-r-i-n-a.

                    MRS. LANNAN
               Very good. Now, what about
               "Fragrance"? Anyone?

The boy who was teasing Grace raises his hand.

                    MRS. LANNAN (CONT'D)

Nick, please.
Nick stands up.

NICK
F-a, no, sorry.

Grace writes down the word accurately on a piece of paper.

NICK (CONT'D)
F-r-a-g-r-a-n-c-e.

MRS. LANNAN
Good job.

Nick sits down, smiling victoriously.

MRS. LANNAN (CONT'D)

Okay, the next one is a bit challenging. "Effervescence" The kids look at each other, nobody figuring it out.

MRS. LANNAN (CONT'D)
No one?

Mrs. Lannan's gaze falls on Grace who's writing the word down on her paper again.

MRS. LANNAN (CONT'D)
Grace.

Grace lifts her head.

MRS. LANNAN (CONT'D)
Can you give it a try?

Grace stands up. Nick sneers covertly.

GRACE

E-f-f-e-r-v-e-s-c-e-n-c-e.

        MRS. LANNAN
Correct! Well done, Grace!

Nick is clearly stung.

INT. CLASSROOM - LATER

Excited students are leaving the classroom.

        MRS. LANNAN
Grace, will you come here for a minute?

Grace moves to Mrs. Lannan's desk.

        MRS. LANNAN (CONT'D)
You're very good at spelling, Grace.

        GRACE
Thank you, Mrs. Lannan.

        MRS. LANNAN
I want you to speak up more from now on.

Grace looks at her teacher whose eyes are piercing behind her glasses.

MRS. LANNAN (CONT'D) You're a very talented girl, Grace.

        Believe in yourself more, okay?
Grace nods unconvincingly.

        MRS. LANNAN (CONT'D)

You know you can be promoted to
the
4th grade so you are able to take two grades together.
        GRACE

>   Really?

                MRS. LANNAN
          Yes. Shall I set up a meeting with
          Mr. Kiracofe, the superintendent?
                He'd love to meet you.

Grace's little face cracks into a wide smile.

EXT. HAZEL'S HOUSE – AFTERNOON

Grace walks up to the house and sees Harold load a suitcase into the trunk of his Chevy.
>   GRACE
>   Where are you going, Dad?

Harold turns, his face impassive.

>   HAROLD
>   Get in. Dinner is ready.

>   GRACE
>   Oh.

>   HAROLD
>   Your mom made elk.

>   GRACE
>   Okay....

Grace pauses for a beat, knowing something's up, then heads into the house. Harold gets into his car and drives away.

INT. KITCHEN/GRACE'S HOME - NIGHT

Grace, Patty (7) and Hazel eat in silence.

>   PATTY
>   Mom, when is Dad coming back?

Hazel says nothing, tear tracks shining on her face.

INT. BEDROOM/HAZEL'S HOUSE - NIGHT

In bed, Patty sobs her heart out. Grace covers her ears with her hands.

>   GRACE
> Stop crying, will you?!

> Patty's whine
> redoubles.
>   PATTY
> I want Dad.

>   GRACE
> Shut up! Just shut up!

EXT. BACKYARD GARDEN/HAZEL'S HOUSE - DAY
Flowers languish. Vegetables turn yellow. The yard is overgrown with weeds.

INT. HAZEL'S BEDROOM/HAZEL'S HOUSE - DAY

Cold gray morning light exposes the room. In bed, Hazel turns away from the window and pulls a blanket over her head.
INT. KITCHEN/HAZEL'S HOUSE - DAY

Grace rummages through the pantry. INT.

KITCHEN/HAZEL'S HOUSE - LATER

Grace mixes flour with water in a bowl.

INT. KITCHEN/HAZEL'S HOUSE - LATER

Grace and Patty eat pancakes made from flour and water. Patty chews and winces in disgust.

                    PATTY
                    Eww.

                    GRACE
                 This is all we have!

EXT. BIG ARM SCHOOL - DAY

Grace rushes into the building

INT. HALLWAY/BIG ARM SCHOOL - DAY

Grace tiptoes to the classroom.
                 MRS. LANNAN (O.S.)
                    Grace.

Grace turns and sees Mrs. Lannan, embarrassed.

                    GRACE
              I'm sorry I'm late, Mrs. Lannan.

                  MRS. LANNAN
              You don't remember we were supposed
              to meet Mr. Kiracofe this morning?

Grace's hands fly to her mouth.

                    GRACE
              Oh, no! I forgot! I'm so
              sorry, Mrs. Lannan....

                  MRS. LANNAN
              You forgot? I thought this
              was important for you,
                    Grace.

                    GRACE
                 It is! I swear.

Mrs. Lannan looks at Grace for a beat and notices that there's flour all over her dress. Mrs. Lannan clasps Grace lightly on the arm.

      MRS. LANNAN
    Is everything okay, Grace?

Grace blinks.

       GRACE
     What do you mean?

      MRS. LANNAN
I want you to know that if you ever need any help, I'm here.
       GRACE
     Everything is fine.

INT. LIVING ROOM/HAZEL'S HOUSE - LATE AFTERNOON

Grace comes home to dirty dishes on coffee table; food has dried and stuck on plates above which a fly buzzes.

INT. KITCHEN/HAZEL'S HOUSE - LATE AFTERNOON

Grace washes all the dirty dishes.

INT. CLASSROOM - DAY

Leanne who's sitting behind Grace sniffs the air.

       LEANNE
     What's that smell?

Grace buries her face in a book, flatten her oily hair as if that could prevent its smell from coming out.

EXT. HAZEL'S HOUSE - NIGHT

Grace carries a bucket of water into the house.

INT. KITCHEN/HAZEL'S HOUSE - NIGHT

Grace washes her hair in a dish pan.

INT. KITCHEN/HAZEL'S HOUSE - LATER

Grace washes Patty's hair.

          GRACE
Have you talked to Mom today?

          PATTY
No. She left with a man. He could be
her Knight On A White Horse.

          GRACE
Right.

          PATTY
Can we take a bath tonight?

          GRACE
We can't. It will take too
long to heat up the water.

          PATTY
I don't want to go to school
smelling like garbage!

          GRACE
Then go ahead and bath
in ice cold water!

Grace throws a small towel at her sister. Patty dries her hair fretfully.

EXT. HAZEL'S HOUSE - DAY

Grace hangs laundry on a line to dry, her face and hands scarlet from the cold.

EXT. HAZEL'S HOUSE - DAY

Grace retreats the clothes which are like stiff boards.

INT. LIVING ROOM/HAZEL'S HOUSE - NIGHT

Grace comes out of the kitchen to Patty.

                    GRACE
          We don't have anything.

Tears swim in Patty's eyes.
                    PATTY
            I'm hungry.

EXT. NEIGHBOR'S HOUSE - NIGHT

Grace knocks on the door. MRS. PARSONS opens and is surprised to see Grace and Patty.

                    GRACE
         Good evening, Mrs. Parsons.

               MRS. PARSONS
       Grace! Patty! What's wrong?
      Are you okay? Where is Hazel?

                    GRACE
       Mom hasn't been back for a
      few days and there's nothing
        to eat in the house....

Grace's voice trails off. A knowing look in Mrs. Parsons eyes.

               MRS. PARSONS
          Come on in, girls.

INT. DINING ROOM/MRS. PARSONS' HOUSE - NIGHT
Grace and Patty sit uncomfortably in their shabby clothes in front of Mrs. Parsons' daughter, EMMA, who's in a beautiful, pink

dress. Emma's cheeks wear a healthy bloom and her exquisite blonde hair shines in the warm light.

Mrs. Parsons brings out spectacular dishes.

> MRS. PARSONS
> (to Grace and Patty)
> Help yourselves.

Patty digs in at once.

> GRACE
> Thank you so much,
> Mrs. Parsons.

Mrs. Parsons gives Grace a smile, sits down and begins to put food onto her daughter's plate. Grace looks at Mrs. Parsons' loving gaze, stalled between sadness and longing.

EXT. CHURCH - DAY SUPER: 1951

Hazel (30s), in a white dress, and LAWRENCE (40s) walk out of a church, their arms entwined. Grace (12) and Patty (10), flowers in their hands and mutinous expression on their faces, follow their mom and new stepdad.

A small crowd of FRIENDS AND FAMILY cheers. Grace feels a hot gaze. She turns and sees a dashing young man (20s) beaming at her. Grace averts her head shyly.

INT. LIVING ROOM/HAZEL'S HOUSE - DAY

Through the window, Grace watches Lawrence open the door of his car for Hazel and playfully grab her butt. Hazel's unctuous laugh makes Grace frown in contempt. The parents drive away.

INT. SCHOOL BUS - MOVING – AFTERNOON
Grace sits alone on the bus. Chuckles from other students drift into her ears.

EXT. HAZEL'S HOUSE - AFTERNOON

Grace walks up to the house and stops suddenly in her tracks. The handsome young man from the wedding is on the porch. He sees Grace and waves.

>YOUNG MAN
>Hi!

Grace is taken aback.

>YOUNG MAN (CONT'D)
>My name is Herb. I was
>at the wedding. I'm your
>dad's friend.

Herb moves closer to Grace and puts out his hand.

>HERB
>Grace, right?

Grace wavers for a beat, then shakes his hand.

>GRACE
>Were you waiting for Lawrence?
>He's gone with my mom. They
>won't be back till Sunday.

>HERB
>Oh, really? Where did they go?

>GRACE
>They didn't mention.

>HERB
>All good. I'm not here for them.

Grace looks at him, puzzled.

>HERB (CONT'D)

                    I'm here for you.

Grace is surprised.
                    HERB (CONT'D)
                         Here.
Herb takes out a chocolate bar from his pocket and hands it to Grace.

                         GRACE
                         For me?

                         HERB
                      Yeah. Take it.

                         GRACE
                      Thank you....

Grace grabs the candy from Herb's hand.

                         HERB
                    I will see you
                    around, Grace.
With those words and a charming smile, Herb takes his leave. Grace looks down at the chocolate in her hand, swiftly suppressing a smile.

            INT. PICK UP TRUCK - MOVING – NIGHT
Patty sits on Grace's lap and Hazel is in the middle by Lawrence who's driving.
                         HAZEL
                  (to Grace and PATTY) That
                  picture was awesome! It was
                  some good family time, wasn't it?

                Don't complain I don't spend
                time with you two anymore.

                         PATTY

Grace wasn't even watching.

Grace shoots her sister a fierce look.

      HAZEL
    You weren't, Grace?

Patty whips out a Zane Grey book out of nowhere.

      GRACE
     (to Patty)
    Give it back!

     LAWRENCE
  How could she read in the dark?

Grace snatches her book back. Hazel looks offended.

      GRACE
     (to Hazel)
 You know I don't like scary movies, Mom.

      PATTY
  (to Grace) That's because you're boring.

      GRACE
     (to Patty)
Well, you're stupid! Incensed, Patty stomps on Grace feet.

     GRACE (CONT'D)
     Ouch!

Patty stomps again.

     GRACE (CONT'D)
    If you do that again,
    I will kill you!

Hazel reaches over and starts pulling Grace's hair.

> HAZEL
> (to Grace) Never say
> that agaitn!

Patty grins.

> HAZEL (CONT'D)
> (to Grace)
> I will put you in reform school
> if you don't behave!

INT. BEDROOM/HAZEL'S HOUSE - NIGHT

Grace lies in bed with tears streaming down her face.

INT. BEDROOM/HAZEL'S HOUSE- DAY

Herb lolls in Grace's bed with a book in hand. Grace sits beside Herb, looking at him with admiration.

> HERB
>
> (reading aloud from the book)
> "A love affair should be a thing of
> silence, soft, unspoken. No raucous voice,
> no burst of sudden laughter, but the kind of stealthy curiosity
> that comes with fear, and when the
> fear has gone, a brazen confidence.
> Never the give-and-take between good friends,
> but passion between strangers...."

> GRACE
>
> Is that how lovers should be?

> HERB
> In my world, yes.

Herb flickers a flirtatious smile. Grace looks perplexed.

> HERB (CONT'D)
> You will understand
> when you're older.

> GRACE
> Don't talk to me like
> I'm a little girl.

Herb puts down his book.

> HERB
> You want me to
> treat you like a woman?

He scans the bedroom.

HERB (CONT'D) Where is your sister?

> GRACE
> Out with friends, I think.

> HERB
> And you don't like to
> hang out with them?

Grace shakes her head.

> GRACE
> I enjoy the
> luxury of solitude.

Herb laughs.

> GRACE (CONT'D)
> I know, I'm no fun.

> HERB

                    I disagree.

Herb looks into Grace's eyes and inches closer.

                    HERB (CONT'D)
                    So, she won't be
                    back for awhile?

                    GRACE
                    Probably. Why?

Herb takes Grace's face in his hands and kisses her lips. Grace pulls away in a surge of panic.
                    HERB
                    I really like you, Grace.

Herb places his hand on Grace's lap, undeterred.

                    GRACE
                    I --

                    HERB
                    You're different; special.

Grace, not knowing what to say, lets Herb stroke her hair.

                    HERB (CONT'D)
                    I know you want to be loved,
                    Grace. Let me give it to you.

Herb starts to kiss Grace passionately and she can't seem to move away. He unbuttons Grace's blouse. Grace's whole frame trembles.

                    HERB (CONT'D)
                    (whispering)
                    It's okay....

EXT. HAZEL'S HOUSE - AFTERNOON

Herb strides to his car, satisfaction and arrogance plain on his face.

INT. BEDROOM/HAZEL'S HOUSE - AFTERNOON

Grace, wrapped in a blanket, looks outside the window blankly, as though waking from a long dream.

INT. CLASSROOM – DAY

Grace stares at an open book in front of her, but her mind is somewhere else. Mrs. Lannan's voice is in the background.

INT. KITCHEN/HAZEL'S HOUSE – NIGHT

The family is having dinner. Grace chances a glance at her stepfather.

GRACE
(to Lawrence)
Have you heard from
your friend, Herb?

Lawrence is surprised while Hazel looks suspicious.

LAWRENCE
Herb?

HAZEL
(to Grace)

Why do you ask about him?
PATTY

(to Grace) You like him,
don't you?

Grace gives Patty a death stare.

HAZEL

(to Grace)
Is that true?

GRACE
That's absolutely not -PATTY

Grace's got a boyfriend!

GRACE
(bellowing)
He's not my --

HAZEL
(to Grace) Do not you raise
your voice!

Grace swallows.

GRACE
(to Lawrence)
He came the other day
and was looking for you.

LAWRENCE
When?

Grace feigns airiness.

GRACE
Last week... but you
guys were gone.

LAWRENCE

Weird. He didn't
mention it before he left.

GRACE
Left?

LAWRENCE

                    Yeah, he left town.

Grace is confounded. She catches Hazel looking at her and hastily rearranges her expression.

EXT. HAZEL'S HOUSE – NIGHT

A zigzag flash of lightning. A crash of thunder. Rain pours down ruthlessly.

INT. BEDROOM/HAZEL'S HOUSE - NIGHT

Grace looks at the rain, blinding thunder-light illuminating her face for one second and complete darkness enshrouding it the next.

INT. LIVING ROOM/HAZEL'S HOUSE – NIGHT

Grace opens the front door and lets the rain drive in upon her. She holds something inside her robe.

EXT. HAZEL'S HOUSE - NIGHT

Grace runs out to the front yard, soaked in an instant. She takes out the thing in her robe - it's a 22 pistol.

Grace sits down on a block of wood and holds the gun to her temple. Tears ooze out of her puffy eyes.

Grace puts her finger on the trigger, her hand shaking uncontrollably. She closes her eyes.
After a long beat, Grace opens her eyes and puts the gun down. Crashed by a deluge of emotions, she cries out loud like she's never cried before. Sheets of rain obscure her tears; rolls of thunder engulf her voice.

EXT. HAZEL'S HOUSE - DAY

Mrs. Lannan, looking concerned, knocks on the door. No one answers.

                    MRS. LANNAN
               Grace? It's Mrs. Lannan.

INT. BEDROOM/HAZEL'S HOUSE - DAY

Grace is in bed.
                    MRS. LANNAN (O.S.)
                         Grace?
Grace ignores her teacher.

INT. BEDROOM/HAZEL'S HOUSE - LATER

Grace grabs a few clothes and stuffs them in a backpack.

EXT. ROAD – DAY

Grace looks at her "home", turns and walks away.
EXT. JANE AND CARL'S HOUSE - DUSK

Jane (60s) opens the door to an exhausted Grace.
                         JANE
               Grace? What are you doing here?
                         GRACE
               I can't live with my mom anymore, Grandma Jane. I
               promise you I will pay you back --

                         JANE
                    Hold on, Child.

Jane looks at Grace from head to toe.

                         JANE (CONT'D)
               Did you walk all the way here?

Grace nods. Mae's face softens.

                         JANE (CONT'D)

> Come in. I will give
> you some water.

INT. SITTING ROOM/JANE AND CARL'S HOUSE - NIGHT

Carl slams the telephone down.

> CARL
> She didn't even look for her.

> JANE
> That can't be true. Grace is --

INT. KITCHEN/JANE AND CARL'S HOUSE - NIGHT

Grace puts down a bowl of soup and listens.

> JANE (O.S.)
> -- her daughter.

> CARL (O.S.)
> You know she never wanted a girl!

> JANE (O.S.) What
> should we do, Carl?

> CARL (O.S.)
> We can't let Grace go
> back to that house.

INT. BEDROOM/JANE AND CARL'S HOUSE - NIGHT

Another stormy night. Grace can't sleep. A gentle knock on the door. Sandy (30s) comes in.

> SANDY
> I saw the light was on.

Sandy sits on the edge of the bed.

> GRACE
> I'm scared.

> SANDY
> Of the storm?

Grace nods.

> SANDY (CONT'D)
> Here, let me tell you a poem and you
> will find the lightening storms are just
> as beautiful as the sunrise.

> GRACE
> Really?

> SANDY
> Lying on my bed, watching the lightening flash,
> across the valley below.
> (MORE)

> SANDY (CONT'D)
> I was spellbound as each flash raced
> over the ground. Horses appeared in the
> bright light then disappeared like
> Ghosts.

Sandy steers Grace by the shoulder so they face the window.

> SANDY (CONT'D)
> The rain came, at first soft but quickly
> became silver sheets against each resplendent
> flash. The thunder's echo grew faint the
> flashes dimmed. I felt a tugging inside
> darkness was back.

Grace's eyes grow heavy. Sandy gives her a kiss on the forehead.

SANDY (CONT'D)
Goodnight, Angel.

MONTAGE BEGINS

INT. DEPARTMENT STORE - DAY

Ray (30s) and his WIFE (30s) take Grace shopping for clothes.

INT. SANDY'S HOME - DAY

Sandy teaches Grace to paint. Delight spreads over Grace's face when she gets her own brushes and experiment different mixture of colors.

EXT. SHEEP RANCH - DAY

Grace helps Carl with the sheep.

INT. KITCHEN/JANE AND CARL'S HOUSE - NIGHT

Grace wolfs down Mae's amazing food.

EXT. SHEEP RANCH - DAY

Grace milks cows.

INT. SANDY'S HOME - NIGHT

Sandy plays a guitar and sings a song. Grace is enchanted by her aunt's voice.

EXT. SHEEP RANCH - DAY

Grace paints the yellow roses that she used to smell as a kid.

EXT. SHEEP RANCH - NIGHT

Grace lies on the grass, watching the magical northern lights.

EXT. HILLS - DAY

Grace rides bareback across the hills, happy and free.

MONTAGE ENDS

INT. SITTING ROOM/JANE AND CARL'S HOUSE - NIGHT

Grace walks into the room to a solemn Jane.

                GRACE
        Is everything alright,
           Grandma Jane?

                JANE
         Patty is leaving.

A beat.

GRACE To where?

JANE Terry. She's going to live with her dad.

Grace doesn't speak.

             JANE (CONT'D)

      Your grandpa and I are
      going to Polson to see
      her off. Your mom will
      be there too. Would you
       like to come with us?

Another beat.

                GRACE
                 No.

INT. TRUCK - MOVING - DAY

SUPER: 1954

Grace (15) drives in a truck that looks more like a big boat. She hums to a song that's on the radio.

INT. THEATRE - DAY

Grace watches *The River Of No Return* alone, her eyes glued to Robert Mitchum's handsome face.

INT. SITTING ROOM/JANE AND CARL'S HOUSE – NIGHT

Carl sips on a cup of tea while Ray reads the papers. Grace marches into the room.

>   GRACE
>   Grandpa Carl.

Carl looks up.

>   CARL
>   Yes, Grace?

>   GRACE
>   I want to go with you.

>   CARL
>   I'm sorry?

>   GRACE
>   I want to go to St.
>   Joe National Forest
>   with the sheep too.

>   RAY
>   No.

>   GRACE

                        (frustrated)
                    But why, Uncle Ray?

                            RAY
                It's dangerous for a young girl to be
                        around the herders.

                           GRACE
                      I can take care of myself.

                            RAY
                       You're only 15.

                           CARL
                         (to Grace)
                      Your uncle is right.
                    You're not coming with me.

Grace, disappointed, stomps upstairs.

INT. KITCHEN/JANE AND CARL'S HOUSE - DAY

SUPER: 1955

Grace approaches Jane when she's prepping for lunch.

                           JANE

                      I don't need your
                        help, Sweetie.

                          GRACE
                  Hmm.... It's something else.

Jane wipes her hands on her apron and looks at Grace.

                      GRACE (CONT'D)

                            49

>   Can you sign this for me?

Grace holds out a piece of paper.

>   JANE
>   What is this?
>
>   GRACE
>   It's... permission to go the Army.

Mae's eyes go wide.

>   GRACE (CONT'D)
>   I'm 16 so... someone have to sign.
>
>   JANE
>   Oh... Sweetie....
>   You know I can't do that.
>
>   GRACE
>   Please, Grandma Jane.
>   I really want to do something with my life!
>
>   JANE
>   I understand. But you're still young.
>   Grace looks defeated.
>
>
>   JANE (CONT'D)
>   Your uncle and your grandpa
>   Would kill me
>   if I signed. I'm sorry.

INT. BEDROOM/JANE AND CARL'S HOUSE - NIGHT

Grace looks despondent as Sandy enters the room.

SANDY
I heard what happened.

Grace's shoulders rise and fall.

SANDY (CONT'D)
Is that really what you want to do?
Join the Army?

GRACE
If I said yes, would you sign for me?

SANDY
Actually, I would.
You know I'd want you to go after your dream.

GRACE
Frankly, I'm not sure if that's my dream...
Aunt Sandy.

Sandy smiles assuringly.

SANDY
It's okay. You're still figuring it out.

Sandy turns to leave.

GRACE
I want to go to college one day.

Sandy looks back at her niece, surprised.

EXT. HALLWAY OUTSIDE BEDROOM/JANE AND CARL'S HOUSE DAY

Jane knocks on the door.

> JANE
> Grace, time for breakfast!

No response.

> JANE (CONT'D)
> Grace?

Jane pushes the door open and is astonished to see an empty room.

INT. BEDROOM/JANE AND CARL'S HOUSE - DAY

Jane picks up a letter on the bed and reads.

> GRACE (V.O.)
> Grandma Jane, I've decided
> to go to Whitefish and look
> for work. Thank you for the last four years.
> It was the best time of my life.

INT. GRACE'S TRUCK - MOVING - DAY

Grace drives past a road sign that says: "Whitefish".

> GRACE (V.O.)
> But I have to learn to be on
> My own. Thank Grandpa Carl,
>
>
> Uncle Ray and Aunt Sandy for me.
> I will miss you guys, and
> I shall cherish my memories
> on the ranch forever.

INT. BAR - DAY

Grace sets foot in a shabby, empty bar with dirty floor and greased tables. She wrinkles her nose.

GRACE
Hello?

A plump woman, JULIA (30s), comes out from the back kitchen.

JULIA
We're closed.

GRACE
Hmm... no... ma'am.
I was wondering if
you need any help here....

JULIA
You're looking for a job

GRACE
Yes, ma'am.

JULIA
How old are you?
GRACE
16.

Julia looks at Grace with interest.

JULIA
I can offer you 75
cents an hour to clean this place.

GRACE
I will take it!

JULIA
Great. Can you start now?

MONTAGE BEGINS

INT. BAR - DAY Grace

wipes down the tables.

Grace sweeps and mops the floor.

INT. BATHROOM/BAR - DAY

Grace, covering her nose with her sleeve, cleans the toilet.
MONTAGE ENDS

INT. BAR - NIGHT

Julia hands Grace some cash.

>   GRACE
>   Thank you so much, ma'am.
>
>   JULIA
>   Call me Julia. Where are you staying?
>   GRACE
>   I'm going to sleep in my truck before figuring something out.
>
>   JULIA
>   Sleep in the truck? A girl like you?
>
>   GRACE
>   I don't know anybody here....
>
>   JULIA
>   You know what, you can stay with me.
>   I have a spare room.
>
>   GRACE

Oh, no, I don't have enough money to pay you.

                JULIA
        Don't worry about it, Kid.
        You're doing a good job here.
          I wanna help you out.

               GRACE
Really, Julia? Oh my god, thank you so much. You
     have no idea how grateful I am.

               JULIA
          Yeah, yeah.

Julia smirks.

          JULIA (CONT'D)
        Oh, just one thing...
I have a son and he still lives with me. And...
     I can't wait for you to meet him.

INT. KITCHEN/JULIA'S HOUSE – DAY
Grace fishes out a bottle of milk from the fridge when ED (20s), a young man with television good looks, walks in. Pinkness suffuses Grace's cheeks instantly.

               GRACE
        Good morning, Ed.

                ED
      Morning. Having a day off?

               GRACE
            Yeah.

Ed pours himself a glass of water.

          GRACE (CONT'D)

>   Emm... I was about to make breakfast.
>   Would you like some?
>
>   ED
>   I'm heading out.
>   Thanks anyway.
>
>   GRACE
>   No worries....

INT. LIVING ROOM/JULIA'S HOUSE - LATER

Grace peers outside the window and sees Ed get into a GIRL's car and share an intimate kiss with her.

INT. DINING ROOM/JULIA'S HOUSE - NIGHT

Grace has dinner with Julia whose expression is dour.

>   JULIA
>   Do you know where Ed is?
>
>   GRACE
>   No....
>
>   JULIA
>   You're not a good liar,
>   Grace. He's at the bar, isn't he?

Grace says nothing. Julia lets out a sigh.

>   JULIA (CONT'D)
>   He's a good kid,
>   but he needs to grow up.
>   If he were to get married,
>   I'm sure he'd mature.

Julia eyes Grace who's fixating her gaze on her plate.

JULIA (CONT'D)
You find him handsome,
don't you, Grace?

GRACE
I... I'm sorry?

JULIA
I know you do.
I see the way you look at him.
Let me tell you something,
Grace.

You're a nice girl. I'd love to have you as my daughter-in-law
Grace looks at Julia in astonishment.

GRACE
Me?

JULIA
You don't drink; you don't smoke,
which means you are perfect for Ed.

A dry laugh from Grace.

GRACE
I really don't think he's gonna want to marry me,
Julia. He's got a girl.

Julia sneers.

JULIA
That bird ain't going to marry my son as
long as I'm still alive!

GRACE
They're in love....

> JULIA
> I know what's best for him, Grace.
> He needs to be set on the right path.
> and I will make sure that happens.

Grace looks at Julia, unsure.

INT. SITTING ROOM/JANE AND CARL'S HOUSE - DAY

Grace holds out her left hand for Jane to see; a small ring on her fourth finger, sparkling in the sunlight.

> JANE
> That's very pretty, Grace.

> GRACE
> Thank you, Grandma Jane.

> JANE
> I'm happy for you.
> Ray and Sandy, on the other hand, assume a skeptical look on their faces.

> RAY
> (to Grace)
> Are you sure you want to get married?

> GRACE
> Of course, I am.

> SANDY
> Have you thought it through, Grace? I mean, we haven't even met the guy. How old is he? What does he do? And --

Jane waves Sandy down while Grace looks bombarded.

                    JANE
Enough. Grace likes the boy and that's all that matters.
        Let herset out on her new life, Sandy.
Montana doesn't have a lot to Offer to young folks, after all.
         Sandy bites her lip, still looking doubtful.

                    GRACE
                  (to Sandy)
         Don't worry about me, Aunt Sandy.
                This is what I want.

INT. WEDDING CHAPEL - DAY

Grace, in a navy blue dress, and Ed, in a black suit, stand in front of a PASTOR.

                    PASTOR
        I now pronounce you husband and wife.

INT. APARTMENT - DAY

Grace looks around in a tiny, grubby apartment with the LANDLADY (40s).
                   LANDLADY
            The bathroom is on the second floor.
              It's shared with all of the tenants.

                    GRACE
                   Okay...

Through the open front door, Grace sees a MAN race down the hallway arms waving and talking incoherently. Grace looks startled.

LANDLADY
Don't mind him. He has delirium tremens.

Apprehension fills Grace's face.

LANDLADY (CONT'D)
Rent is due on the first. I will charge late fee if you're late.
Deposit is not required. Any other questions?

INT. APARTMENT - LATER

Grace cleans the stove.

INT. APARTMENT - LATER

Grace opens a cupboard and screams as cockroaches scurry away in every direction.

INT. APARTMENT - NIGHT

Grace, alone in bed, looks at a clock. The dim roar of the city can be heard in the background.

INT. BAR - NIGHT

Ed drinks with his FRIENDS. They roar with laughter, having a fabulous time.

INT. APARTMENT - DAY

Grace and Ed sit at the table, having lunch.

GRACE
The landlady says she will give me a job
cleaning some of the apartments.
It's something, right?

ED
Sure.

Ed gulps down the last bits of his food and leaps up from his chair.

GRACE
You're going out again?

ED
Yeah, gonna see some friends.

Grace's face darkens.

GRACE
You are still looking for work, aren't you?

ED
Come on, Grace, don't act like my mom.

MONTAGE BEGINS

EXT. STREET - AFTERNOON

Grace, in a plain summer dress, walks down the street.

EXT. THEATRE - AFTERNOON

Grace goes into the theatre.

EXT. THEATRE - LATER

The sun sinks to the level of the treetops outside the theatre. The billboard lights up. Grace reemerges onto the street.

INT. APARTMENT - NIGHT

Grace eats dinner alone.

EXT. PARK - DAY

Grace, a baby bump under her knitted sweater, saunters in a park. Sun rays stream down through a canopy of dark red leaves.

INT. THEATRE - AFTERNOON

Grace watches *Gone With The Wind*, chewing on a Snicker Bar.

EXT. STREET - NIGHT

Grace walks home on the twilit road.

MONTAGE ENDS

INT. HALLWAY/HOSPITAL – DAY
Ed paces up and down in the hallway. He jumps when a door is pushed open and a NURSE comes out.

                    NURSE
          Congratulations. It's a boy.

INT. ROOM/HOSPITAL - DAY

Grace, lying in a hospital bed, holds a baby boy, CHAD, in her arms. She looks at him with the most tender fondness.

INT. KITCHEN/APARTMENT - DAY

Grace cooks with Chad in her arm. A knock on the door.

INT. HALLWAY OUTSIDE APARTMENT - DAY

Grace opens the door and is stunned into silence. In front of her stands Patty (15).

                    PATTY
                   Hi, Grace.

INT. KITCHEN/APARTMENT – DAY
Patty beams down at Chad who's in his crib.

                    PATTY
                   Cute boy.

Grace hands Patty a glass of water.

                    GRACE

         I thank god for giving me a boy.
         If Chad had been a girl, I probably
            would have sent him back.

                    PATTY
         You wouldn't be that cruel, Grace.
                 It's not in you.

                    GRACE
                  Well, I would.

The sisters stand in strained silence for a moment.

                 GRACE (CONT'D)
              Why don't you sit down?

They sit down at the table, face to face. Patty takes a sip of her water. An awkward beat.
                    PATTY
             Gosh, how long has it been?

                    GRACE

Three years.

PATTY
I was mad at you for not coming to see me off.

GRACE
I'm sorry, Patty.
I couldn't face Mom.

Patty takes another sip of water.

PATTY
How are you?

GRACE
I'm good. Ed has finally got a job as a
car cleaner with Rock Island Railroad.
And I'm working as a housekeeper.

PATTY
Are you happy?

Grace is taken aback. Patty's eyes scan the apartment.

PATTY (CONT'D)
I mean, is this your happy home?

GRACE
The apartment is temporary.
We don't have money to buy a house yet.
But I want to get a second job and save up.

PATTY
You have it all planned out.

GRACE
What about you? Are you happy?

A hallow smile appears on Patty's face.

                    PATTY
            Me? I don't think I will ever
              know what happiness is.

A pause.

                    GRACE
              I know what happened in
              the cherry orchard, Patty.

Patty sits quietly, staring at Grace.

                    PATTY
               I don't know what
                you're talking about.

The sisters look at each other for a beat. Grace suddenly stands up and walks to the sink.

                    GRACE
              I'm glad you came. You
            should spend the summer here.
                What do you say?

Patty gazes mistily at the particles that are dancing in the air.

                    PATTY
        Yeah... Grace....That sounds like a good idea.

INT. BEDROOM/APARTMENT - NIGHT - THREE MONTHS LATER

Grace, sitting on the bed, folds diapers with Chad on her side. A horrible explosion-like noise. Chad starts to cry.

                    GRACE
                (voice quivering)
                     Ed?

                    ED (O.S.)
                    What?

Ed comes out of the bathroom, hair wet and wearing a robe.
                    GRACE
                    You didn't hear that noise?

                    ED
                    What noise?

                    GRACE
                    It was the airplane.
                    It was so close to us!
            I thought it was flying into the building!

                    ED
                    Don't be ridiculous.

Grace takes Chad in her arms.

                    GRACE
                I hate the city. All the traffic...
                and I'm terrified of the planes!

                    ED
                    Stop with the planes!
Ed walks out of the bedroom.
ED (O.S.) (CONT'D) What the.... Hey, Grace! Come out here!

INT. KITCHEN/APARTMENT - NIGHT

Grace is astounded to see the state of her kitchen: macaroni is on the ceiling, walls and floor. Ed stands next to a pressure cooker and looks at her with his arms tightly crossed.

                    ED
            Did you make macaroni In the pressure cooker?

The look on Grace's face confirms it.

> ED (CONT'D)
> It plugged the vent!
> What were you thinking?

> GRACE
> I'm sorry....

Grace begins to clean the mess wordlessly.

> ED
> What if Chad was in here?
> Airplanes.... Unbelievable.

INT. BEDROOM/APARTMENT - DAY

SUPER: 1960
Grace (19) irons Chad's socks and baby clothes, her stomach protruding. Chad (2) plays on the floor.

> GRACE
> (to Chad)
> Are you ready to meet your little brother?

Chad looks up at his mom, a big smile on his adorable face.

> GRACE (CONT'D)
> Yes? Momma too.
> We definitely don't want a sister, do we?

MONTAGE BEGINS

INT. HOSPITAL ROOM - DAY

Grace nurses her newborn, CHARLES.

EXT. COMO PARK - DAY

Grace take the boys to see wild animals.

INT. CAR/DRIVE IN THEATER - NIGHT

Chad, in his pajamas, watches a movie on the sliver screen. Grace cradles Charles while keeping up with the plot.

MONTAGE ENDS

INT. BEDROOM/APARTMENT - NIGHT

Grace is reading when she notices that Charles (1) is listless. Panic-stricken, she sees that his fingernails are blue. Grace grabs the phone and dials a number. No one picks up. She dials another number.

                        JULIA (O.S.)
                            Grace?

                            GRACE
Julia! Something is wrong with Charles!
                            (MORE)

                        GRACE (CONT'D)
           His nails are turning blue.
             I don't know what to do!
Ed is at work and won't pick up his phone.

                        JULIA (O.S.)
Get Charles to the hospital as fast as you can!
            I will stay with Chad.

INT. HOSPITAL ROOM - NIGHT

A NURSE places Charles in a hospital crib. Grace looks at her son who looks like he has fallen asleep.

                            GRACE
             Is he going to be okay?!

> NURSE
> Please wait outside, ma'am.

The nurse's face suddenly blanches.

> NURSE (CONT'D)
> Oh, no.

> GRACE
> What is it?!

DR. BRUSEGARD bolts in.

> NURSE
> (to Dr. Brusegard)
> He stopped breathing.

> GRACE
> (horrified) What?!

Dr. Brusegard quickly performs infant CPR. Grace bursts into tears.

> DR. BRUSEGARD
> Please calm down, ma'am.
> I've retrieved his heartbeat. Your
> baby is going to be alright.

INT. HALLWAY/HOSPITAL - NIGHT

Ed rushes in and skids to a halt in front of his dewy-eyed wife.

> ED
> Is he okay?

> GRACE
> Where were you?!
> I called you 50 times!

ED
I was... at work.

GRACE
This late?
Anxiousness mingled with embarrassment on Ed's face. Grace blinks.

GRACE (CONT'D)
Were you at the bar?

Ed looks down.

GRACE (CONT'D)
I can't believe it,
Ed! You told me you quit!

ED
It was a friend's birthday.
I couldn't get out of it.

GRACE
Your friend?! Your son almost died!

ED
I'm sorry! Alright?!
How's Charles?
What did the doctor say?

GRACE
He has pneumonia.
The doctor did an X-ray. He's going to be fine.

ED
Thank god!

GRACE
Can you ask your boss to give you your paycheck earlier this month? We need to pay the bill and medicine.

ED

I already asked for it....

GRACE
That's great!

ED
And I used it.

GRACE
You what?

ED
I just bought a Ford –

GRACE
Wait, what?!

ED
Mom and I were going to tell you –

GRACE
Julia knows about this?!
Grace closes her eyes, takes big heaving breaths,
trying to calm herself down.

ED
Don't be mad. I will work double shifts next month.
When can we see Charles?

Grace opens her eyes, looking at Ed coldly.

GRACE
I will see him. You won't.

ED
What are you talking about?

                    GRACE
            I'm taking the boys to my grandparents'.

Ed stops dead, shocked by the announcement.

                    GRACE (CONT'D)
            I thought you'd change but I was wrong.

                    ED
            You can't do this. I'm their dad!

                    GRACE
            An incompetent one!

                    ED
            I promise you I won't go drinking
            again. I will sell the car!

Ed looks at Grace imploringly.

                    GRACE
    I'm sorry, but your promise doesn't mean anything to me any-
    more. And please don't try to stop me. I will call the police if
                you do. Goodbye, Ed.

Grace turns on her heels. Ed clenches his fists, rage breaking over him.

                    ED
            This ain't over, woman! I swear!
        I'm gonna tell my mom and you will lose everything!!!

INT. TRAIN - MOVING - DAY

Grace, Chad by her side and Charles in her arms, sit on a train. The MAN sitting across her holds out a newspaper which bores the headline: "President Kennedy shot dead."

INT. SITTING ROOM/JANE AND CARL'S HOUSE - NIGHT

Grace comes into the room to Jane (70s).

> JANE
> Did the boys go to bed?

Grace, nodding, sits down on the couch next to her grandma.

> GRACE
> They fell asleep right away.
> The journey tired them out.
>
> JANE
> They are good-looking boys; especially Chad. He's going to be very handsome, I tell you.
>
> GRACE
> Thanks, Grandma Jane.
>
> JANE
> I talked to your grandpa.
> He's going to sell a cow and cover Charles' hospital bills.
>
> GRACE
> I don't know what to say.... I
> Will pay you and Grandpa Carl back.

Tears sparkle in Grace's eyes.

> JANE
> Don't worry about it, Child. And,
> Happy Birthday. I can't Believe you're 23 already.

INT. BEDROOM/JANE AND CARL'S HOUSE - DAY

Grace looks out the window and watches Chad and Charles play in the snow with Sandy's CHILDREN.

The telephone downstairs rings.

                SANDY (O.S.)
            (from downstairs) Hello?
                 (beat) Hold on.

Sandy's footsteps draw nearer.

          SANDY (O.S.) (CONT'D)
         (from outside the bedroom)
              Grace? It's Ed.

INT. SITTING ROOM/JANE AND CARL'S HOUSE – DAY

Grace is on the phone with Ed.
              ED (ON THE PHONE)
          If you don't come home,
      I will take the kids away from you forever!

                  GRACE
        And how are you going to that?
           I'm not the one who
        has a problem with alcohol!

                    ED
             (ON THE PHONE)
My mom is hiring a lawyer! You will regret it, Grace. I'm telling you -Grace hangs up with distaste. She hears a car stopping outside.

The front door opens and someone walks in. A familiar voice makes Grace jaw drop.

                HAZEL (O.S.)
                   Mom?

Hazel (50s) appears in front of Grace, wearing tawdry clothes and hand in hand with a 19-year-old BOY. Grace looks at them, floored.

                    HAZEL (CONT'D)
                    Oh. It's you.

Hazel looks indifferently at her daughter.

                    HAZEL (CONT'D)
                    How have you been?

INT. SITTING ROOM/JANE AND CARL'S HOUSE - LATER
Jane, on the couch, watches Grace pace blindly around the room.

                    GRACE
                    What's she doing here?!

                    JANE
                    She moved in next door.

                    GRACE
                    Why?!

                    JANE
                    Grace, please sit down.

                    GRACE
              Why does she have to come back into my life?!

                    JANE
                    She's your mom --

                    GRACE
                    I hate being around her.
              And who's that guy? He's her new boyfriend,
                    isn't he? Of course, she'd find
                       someone younger than me!

Jane sighs.
                    JANE

> If only she would
> have had a boy....

GRACE
What?

JANE
Don't you understand? That young
man is just like a son to her.

Grace is appalled.

JANE (CONT'D)
Grace, your mom will never change.
Maybe it's time to accept her for who she is.

GRACE
She disgusts me.

Grace stalks off.

INT. BEDROOM/JANE AND CARL'S HOUSE - NIGHT

Grace, lying in bed, seethes silently in the dark.

EXT. JANE AND CARL'S HOUSE - DAY

Grace's hoeing in the garden when her neighbor, SALLY, a bubbly girl of about Grace's age, stops by.

SALLY
Hey, Grace.

GRACE
Hi, Sally. What's up?

SALLY
You wanna go out on New Years
Eve with me and my friends?

GRACE

Where're you guys going?

SALLY
Just the bar in town.

GRACE
You know I don't drink. Sorry.

SALLY
All good. Oh, your mom moved in next door, right?
Ask her for me, will you? She and her
friend seem to like to have fun. And... he is really cute.
Sally winks. Grace flies into a temper.

SALLY (CONT'D)
See ya.

GRACE
Wait!

MONTAGE BEGINS

INT. BAR - NEW YEAR'S EYE

Grace walks into a bar saturated with raucous people. She follows Sally and a few GUYS to the bar.

Sally coaxes her into taking a shot. Grace gages on the burning sensation.

Grace, tipsy, takes more shots. An older guy, DALE (40s) watches her with interest.

Dale walks over to Grace and leads her onto the dance floor. Grace dances with the stranger, their bodies pressed tightly together.

INT. CAR - NIGHT

Dale kisses Grace eagerly, his hands searching inside her blouse.

MONTAGE ENDS

INT. HOSPITAL - DAY

SUPER: 1963

Sandy (30s) and Grace are waiting outside an office. A DOCTOR opens the door and greets them. Sandy gives Grace an encouraging look before Grace follows him inside.

INT. BEDROOM/JANE AND CARL'S HOUSE - DAY

Grace sits on the bed, her eyes out of focus; her hands on her stomach.

          SANDY (O.S.)
       Are you okay, Grace?
Grace wrenches herself back to reality and gives her aunt an artificial smile.

         SANDY (CONT'D)
   You know you can just go back to Ed.
      He doesn't have to know.

            GRACE
   I can't tell a lie like this. Plus,
       Ed and I are over.

A crease appears on Sandy's forehead.

            SANDY
    Are you sure? You have
   two kids and now you're –

            GRACE
  I thought I could create a perfect family,
Aunt Sandy. I really did. I had seen your marriage and Uncle

Ray's and they seem so perfect. I wanted to mimic yours. But I didn't know the power of alcohol.

Sandy falls silent.

> GRACE (CONT'D)
> I believed I could manage everything
> including an alcoholic husband.
> But I can't do it anymore.
> I need to protect my children.

> SANDY
> But can you protect *three* on your
> own? At least with Ed --

> GRACE
> I've made up my mind.

EXT. JULIA'S HOUSE - DAY

Grace walks up to the house and sees a bright red Ford sitting in the drive way with one side entirely smashed. Grace looks at it with reproof.

INT. LIVING ROOM/JULIA'S HOUSE - DAY

Grace sits on the couch across an irascible Ed.

> ED
> Didn't know you could afford an attorney.

> GRACE
> My grandpa gave me some money.

> ED
> When was your family when we needed the money?

> GRACE

> I wasn't going to embarrass myself in
> front of them just because you had too
> much to drink and couldn't grow up!

Ed grunts.

> ED
> Why are you here?

> GRACE
> You know why, Ed.
> I haven't received this month money.

> ED
> I'm not going to give
> you 80 bucks a month!

> GRACE
> It's your duty to pay child support!
> Your mom already took all the furniture
> and we barely have anything to eat!

> ED
> That's not my problem.

Grace is furious.

> GRACE
> Then you will go to jail!

> ED
> I'd rather sit in a cell than
> giving my money to you!

Grace looks at her ex-husband, astounded.

> ED (CONT'D)
> Now, get out!

INT. KITCHEN/APARTMENT - NIGHT

Grace cooks canned green beans and chicken. Her baby girl, JENNY, cries in a crib.

GRACE
Mommy will feed you soon, okay?

INT. KITCHEN/APARTMENT - LATER

Grace gives Jenny a scant amount of milk while Charles (3) and Chad (5) eat their dinner at the table.

CHARLES
Mommy, we need to get her
some teeth when we go to the store next time.

Grace bursts out laughing.

INT. BATHROOM/APARTMENT - NIGHT

Grace washes bedding and diapers, her hands red and raw.

INT. THE SALVATION ARMY - DAY
Grace is given a wringer washer, children clothing, household goods and a radio.

INT. BEDROOM/APARTMENT - DAY

Grace listens to Dr. Norman Vincent Peale on the radio.

DR. PEALE (O.S.)
(on the radio)
"This is the day which the
Lord hath made;
let us rejoice and be glad in it".

DREAM SEQUENCE BEGINS

EXT. HAZEL'S HOUSE - NIGHT

8-year-old Grace, in battered clothes, stands staring at her childhood home which looks eerie against the velvety blackness of the night.

INT. GRACE'S CHILDHOOD HOUSE - NIGHT

Grace walks in to discover that the house is empty.

                    GRACE
                    Mom?

No reply. Grace runs upstairs.

INT. GRACE'S OLD BEDROOM - NIGHT

Grace dashes into her room which is now vacant.
                    GRACE
                    Patty?
Only silence greets her. Grace breaks down, weeping.

                GRACE (CONT'D)
          Please.... Please don't leave me....

DREAM SEQUENCE ENDS

INT. BEDROOM/APARTMENT - DAWN - PRESENT DAY

Grace wakes up with a yelp of fear.

INT. KITCHEN/JANE AND CARL'S HOUSE - DAY

Grace prepares lunch when Jane cradles Jenny in her arms.

                    JANE
        Since you have three children,
   Try to find an older man that will care for you and them.

GRACE
If a man wanted to take the responsibility of me and three children, he would be out of his mind!

JANE
You'd be surprised, Grace. You still got youth in you. It won't be hard to find a nice guy and remarry.

GRACE
I hardly go out, Grandma Jane.
I don't meet people.

JANE
What about Jenny's father?

GRACE
He doesn't know a thing.
JANE
You should ask Sally. Maybe she knows him. He might be hoping to hear from you. You never know.

INT. CAFE - DAY

Grace is face to face with Dale.

DALE
I didn't expect you to call.
I'm really glad.
Grace smiles.
GRACE
I'm sorry that I didn't reach out sooner and tell you the truth.

DALE
It's not too late.

GRACE
I understand if you want nothing

to do with me.
I have two other small
children with my first husband --

DALE
I love kids.

GRACE
You do?

DALE
Oh, yeah. Always have.
Sally told me about your first husband.

Dale tosses his hand reprovingly.
DALE (CONT'D)
I'm a Korean War Vet, so I can't stand a man who runs away
from his responsibility

GRACE
He's more like a boy himself still.

DALE
I'd gladly care for your kids, Grace.

GRACE
If you don't mind me asking, what do you do?

DALE
I'm a journeyman painter. Money is not an issue, you know,
being a War Vet. I will provide for you guys.

GRACE
Really?

DALE
You don't have to worry anymore, Grace.
Hope radiates from Grace's face.

INT. CHURCH - DAY

SUPER: 1965

The double doors of a church fling open. Grace, backlit by the sublime summer sun, walks down the aisle, holding Carl's arm. Jane, Sandy who's holding Jenny, Ray (40s) and Grace's boys are seated in the crowd. At the end of the aisle, Dale, looking dapper, awaits.

INT. FARM HOUSE – DAY

Dale leads Grace and her kids into a dilapidated farm house. Grace looks around, taking in the state of her new home. Chad and Charles don't look enthusiastic at all.

DALE
It belonged to my aunt.
Pretty spacious, huh?

GRACE
Is there a washer?

DALE
Don't think so.

GRACE
How will I wash clothes then?

DALE
Just carry the water.

GRACE
But it will be freezing cold!

DALE
Oh, there's an electric wand.
Just heat the water with it.

INT. BEDROOM/FARM HOUSE - NIGHT

Grace, sleeping next to Dale, feels something brush over her legs. She sits up, narrowing her eyes in the dark. A mouse runs across the bed. Grace lets out a bellow of terror. Dale startles awake.

DALE
Stay where you are or I will shoot!

GRACE
Dale!

DALE
Huh? What?

GRACE
There's a mouse!

DALE
Oh.... Don't worry, I will get rid of it.

Grace jumps out of bed.

DALE (CONT'D)
Where are you going?

GRACE
I'm gonna check on Jenny!
She'd be scared to death
if there were more of them.

INT. BASEMENT/FARM HOUSE - DAY

Grace puts up a clothesline and hangs washed clothes. When she's just about to finish, the line collapses and everything falls on the dirty floor. Grace takes a deep breath to stop herself from firing up.

GRACE
I will think about this tomorrow.
Yes, that's what I'm going to do.

INT. KITCHEN/FRAM HOUSE - NIGHT

Grace looks into an almost empty fridge when Dale walks in.

                    GRACE
            We're out of groceries.
        Do we have money to get more tomorrow?

                    DALE
            I will manage some through
            The veterans' organization.
            You know, cus I'm a Korean --

                    GRACE
            Korean War Vet. I get it.
            Terrific. Make sure you get
            enough for the five of us.
Dale slumps down in a chair.

                GRACE (CONT'D)
            How was work?

                    DALE
            I got fired.

Grace looks at him in disbelief.

INT. BEDROOM/FARM HOUSE - NIGHT

Dale is in bed. Grace, on the other hand, paces up and down around the room, infuriated.
                    GRACE
            What do you mean the
            boys should move out?!

                    DALE
            Well, they can live with their dad.
            He needs to be responsible, doesn't
            he? And doesn't he have a mother
            to help him out? I can't possible feed

all of us now that I've lost my job.

> GRACE
> And whose fault is that?

> DALE
> I'm a good painter! I'm gonna try my own business.
> Just let Chad and Charles go
> live with Ed for a while.

> GRACE
> How could you ask me to do such a thing?
> You know how careless Ed is!

> DALE
> There's no other way then!
> Unless you want all of us to go back on welfare!

EXT. FARM HOUSE – NIGHT

Grace sits on the front porch, torn. A blanket is put over her body. She turns and sees Chad.

> GRACE
>
> Why aren't you in bed, Sweetie?
>
> CHAD
> I heard your conversation with him.

Grace struggles to find words.

> CHAD (CONT'D)
> It's okay, Mom. Me and
> Charles can go live with Dad.

> GRACE
> No, Chad.

> CHAD
> I know he doesn't care for me, or Charles.

                        GRACE
                    (unconvincingly)
                    That's not true.

                         CHAD
        I can feel it. I'm not happy living here, Mom.
            I'm old enough to take care of Charles.
              You shouldn't worry about if there's
              milk for Jenny or not. Just say yes.
                     I promise we'll be okay.

Grace looks at her son with tear-dimmed eyes and hugs him tightly.
MONTAGE BEGINS

EXT. FARM HOUSE - DAY

Chad and Charles each gives Grace a kiss and get in a car with Ed. Grace watches them drive away, her hand raised in farewell.

INT. A RESIDENCES' HOUSE - DAY

Dale paints a residences' house in town. Grace works with him. She learns quickly and does a fantastic job.

INT. NEW HOUSE - DAY

SUPER: 1966

Grace, a newborn, KYLE, in her arms, motions a MOVER where to put her new furnitures.

EXT. BACKYARD/GRACE AND DALE'S HOUSE - DAY
Jenny (3) runs merrily in a big backyard.

INT. DAYCARE - DAY

A childcare teacher, EMILY (30s), shows Grace around a daycare center which has a roomy upstairs with a kitchen and a bathroom.

Grace looks pleased with the clean environment.

MONTAGE ENDS

INT. BATHROOM/GRACE AND DALE'S HOUSE - NIGHT

Dale, hands trembling, opens a prescription bottle labelled as "Chlordiazepoxide".

                    GRACE (O.S.)
                    Dale?

Dale swallows a couple of pills with some tap water. Grace walks in.

                    GRACE (CONT'D)
                    What are you doing?

Dale ignores Grace who stares down at what's in his hand.

                    GRACE (CONT'D)
                    Didn't the doctor say to only
                    take them in the morning?

Grace takes the pills from Dale, her eyes popping in shock.

                    GRACE (CONT'D)
                    Is this all there's left?
                    How much have you been taking?

Dale waves dismissively.
                    DALE
                    Needed it.

                    GRACE
                    I think you should talk to the doctor.

                    DALE

It's my nerves!
You know they were damaged because of the war!

           GRACE
You are taking way more than prescribed.
It's dangerous -DALE
I'm alright, damn it!
Dale storms away.

INT. BEDROOM/RESIDENCES' HOUSE - DAY

Dale, in a bad mood, paints a wall. His CLIENT saunters in.
           CLIENT
Morning, Dale.
Where's Grace?

           DALE
She had to drop the kids off at daycare.

           CLIENT
Oh, nice, nice. Is she coming to help out later?

           DALE
She sure is.

           CLIENT
Wonderful. Wonderful.

INT. KITCHEN/RESIDENCES' HOUSE - LATER
Dale gets himself some water.

           CLIENT (O.S.)
(in a low voice) God knows
when she will come.

Dale moves over to a door that's open a crack and sees his client talking to his WIFE.

CLIENT'S WIFE (O.S.)
I know. Grace does such a good job.
She's young and precise, unlike him....
Dale's expression sharpens.

CLIENT'S WIFE (O.S.) (CONT'D)
Seriously don't know why he's doing it himself.
He should hire more people or
just let Grace take over the whole thing.
CLIENT (O.S.)
I would! Their reputation
is good because of her.
Dale tightens his grip, as if he were about to smash the glass in pieces.

CLIENT'S WIFE (O.S.)
I'd never hire him if he didn't have her.
He got lucky.

INT. CAR - DAY

Dale slams the door shut, his lips twitching in rage. He bangs his head hard on the steering wheel again and again. His car horns again and again.

INT. DAYCARE – DAY

Emily changes diapers for Kyle and Jenny plays with other KIDS.

Dale charges into the room with a gun in his hand. Emily screams.
EMILY
What are you doing?!

DALE
You wanna see what I can do?!

Dale points his gun at the teacher; he has the eye of a mad man.

                DALE (CONT'D)
              You think I'm a loser?!
       I'm gonna show you I'm not a fool!
INT. LIVING ROOM/GRACE AND DALE'S HOUSE – DAY

Grace is ready to leave for work when the telephone rings. She picks it up and listens, thunderstruck.

INT. POLICE STATION - DAY

Grace sits at a POLICE OFFICER'S desk.

                    OFFICER
            Fortunately, no one was hurt.

                    GRACE
           Thank god. How are my children?

                    OFFICER
          They are safe with their teacher.

                    GRACE
              Thank you, Officer,
           for getting there in time....
The officer barely nods.

                 GRACE (CONT'D)
                And, my husband --

                    OFFICER
              We're not charging him,
     since the daycare has decided to drop the matter.
Not surprised. Who'd want to go there if something like this got
                       out.
                    GRACE
                    True....

                    OFFICER

> I will bring your husband.
> Wait here.

The police officer leaves momentarily, then comes back with Dale.
> OFFICER (CONT'D)
> (to Grace) Good day, ma'am.

> GRACE
> Thank you.

Dale sits down. Grace gives him a burning look.

> GRACE (CONT'D)
> I'm filing for divorce.

> DALE
> What?!

> GRACE
> This is all I can take.

> DALE
> I didn't hurt nobody!

> GRACE
> I've had enough, Dale!
> I sent my boys away because you didn't have a dime!
> My children you promised to care for didn't a pot to pee in,
> or a window to throw it out of!

> DALE
> Grace, please. You can't leave me.

Tears pour down on Dale's lined face, but Grace is unshakeable.
> GRACE
> You know your way home.

She huffs off.

INT. ROOM/GRACE AND DALE'S HOUSE - NIGHT

Grace is packing Jenny and Kyle's clothes.

JENNY
Where are we going, Mommy?

GRACE
Somewhere safe.
The phone rings from downstairs.

GRACE (CONT'D)
I will be right back.

INT. LIVING ROOM/GRACE AND DALE'S HOUSE – NIGHT

Grace answers the call.

GRACE
Hello?

WOMAN
(on the phone etc.) Mrs. Moreno?

GRACE
Yes?

WOMAN
Your husband is in the hospital.

GRACE
What?

WOMAN
He shot himself.

Grace's eyes go wide.

INT. HOSPITAL ROOM - DAY

Dale sleeps in a hospital bed, his cheeks hollow and face wan.

A large bandage wraps around his leg. Grace looks at him, guilt written all over her face.

INT. LIVING ROOM/GRACE AND DALE'S HOUSE - DAY

Grace holds Kyle in one arm and thumbs through a phonebook with her free hand. She locates a number and picks up the phone.

      MAN
    (on the phone etc.)
      Hello?

      GRACE
    Hi! Is this Ralph?

      RAPLH
    Yes. Who's this?

      GRACE
  My name's Grace. I'm Dale's wife.

      RAPLH
  Oh, hello! How's Dale doing?

      GRACE
    Not good actually....
    He's in the hospital.

      RAPLH
    Oh, no. Is he okay?

      GRACE
    He's recovering.
I know you live in Viroqua, but I was wondering if you would come and visit him.
He really needs a friend now.
He always talks a bout his days with you in the war.

      RAPLH

                    What war?

                    GRACE
                Erh... The Korean War?

                    RAPLH
                I was in the Korean War.
                Dale has never set foot in Asia!
Grace is nonplused.
                    GRACE
What? He told me all these stories --
                    RAPLH
                I told him about my time there a
                    and sent him pictures.
                I can't believe he used it to sway girls!

INT. HOSPITAL ROOM - DAY

Grace feeds Dale soup wordlessly.

INT. LIVING ROOM/GRACE AND DALE'S HOUSE - NIGHT

Grace comes home to Sandy.

                    SANDY
                I just tucked them in.

                    GRACE
                Thank you, Aunt Sandy.

                    SANDY
Don't mention it. I love Kyle and Jenny. Grace throws herself into the couch, drained.

                    SANDY (CONT'D)
                Is it true that they were
                Kicked out by the daycare?

97

Grace nods wearily.

                    GRACE
          The entire town knows what
       Dale has done and his suicide attempt.

Sandy sits down next to Grace.

                    SANDY
           This guy is unstable.
          You need to leave him, Grace

                    GRACE
       I can't. He's in the hospital
            because of me.

                    SANDY
  You feel guilty? Or are you afraid of being alone?

Grace looks away.

INT. BEDROOM/GRACE AND DALE'S HOUSE - NIGHT

Grace stirs in her sleep.

DREAM SEQUENCE BEGINS

INT. HAZEL'S HOUSE - NIGHT

8-year-old Grace runs crying in the empty house.

                    GRACE
              Mom? Patty?

DREAM SEQUENCE ENDS

INT. BEDROOM/GRACE AND DALE'S HOUSE - MORNING

Grace wakes up, shriving. The grey morning light floods the room.

MONTAGE BEGINS

EXT. HOSPITAL - DAY

Grace wheels Dale out of the hospital.

INT. BEDROOM/GRACE AND DALE'S HOUSE - DAY

Grace helps Dale get into the bed.

INT. KITCHEN/GRACE AND DALE'S HOUSE - NIGHT

Grace cooks for her kids and her husband.

INT. BEDROOM/GRACE AND DALE'S HOUSE – NIGHT

Grace brings Dale dinner and his pills.

MONTAGE ENDS

INT. LIVING ROOM/GRACE AND DALE'S HOUSE - DAY

After abortive effort to walk, Dale smashes his tea cup on the floor willfully. Grace rushes in.

>   GRACE
>   What happened?

Dale sits back in his wheelchair. Grace looks at ruins of the cup.

>   GRACE (CONT'D)
>   Why did you do that for?

>   DALE
>   Sick of not being able to do anything!

>   GRACE
>   Recovery takes time.

Grace cleans up the mess.

>   GRACE (CONT'D)
>   Lunch is in the fridge.
>   Kyle and Jenny are with my aunt.
>   I'm leaving for work.

Dale grunts irritably.

EXT. HOUSE - DAY

Grace paints a house, continuing the business.

INT. LIVING ROOM/GRACE AND DALE'S HOUSE - DAY

Grace comes back home with Jenny and Kyle who's in a baby carrier. They see that Dale is in the same position except that he's surrounded by innumerable empty beer bottles.

>   GRACE
>   (to Jenny) Come on,
>   let's go upstairs.

Grace takes her daughter's hand and they hurry upstairs. Dale, eyes dim, seems not to notice them. After a moment, Grace comes back down, writhing in rage.

>   GRACE (CONT'D)
>   What's wrong with you?!

Grace's eyes rove around on Dale's face, searching for a reaction.

>   GRACE (CONT'D)
>   Drinking at home? Are you
>   Out of your mind!? You know how
>   I feel about alcohol!

Grace kneels down, picking up the bottles.
GRACE (CONT'D)

> Think about my kids!
> This is not the scene I want them to
> come home to! I can't believe
> I was wooed by your lies.
> Money? The war? You had nothing!

All of a sudden, Dale straightens up, raises his enormous hand and strikes Grace hard across the face, throwing her off balance. Grace covers her flame-like cheek, dumbstruck.

INT. BEDROOM/GRACE AND DALE'S HOUSE - DAY

Grace gets dressed in silence, her face still pink. Dale, leaned upon his elbow on the bed, peers at Grace with shame and regret.

> DALE
> I'm sorry.
> I have no clue how I got that drunk.
> I was just so mad
> at myself. Please forgive me.

> GRACE
> It's too late, Dale.

> DALE
> I promise you it will never happen again, please....

> GRACE
> Me and the kids will leave tonight.
> I will pack our things after work.

> DALE
> Don't do this, Grace!
> Don't threaten me again.

> GRACE
> I'm not threatening you!

And if you're thinking about hurting
yourself again so you can keep me
here, don't even attempt it!
You will have no one's
sympathy this time!

Dale looks beseechingly at Grace, his eyes filled with tears.

                DALE
Please... Grace....
I can't live without you.... Please!

Grace stomps out of the room.

INT. LIVING ROOM/GRACE AND DALE'S HOUSE – AFTERNOON

Grace walks into the house and with parted lips and frightened eyes, sees Kyle sleeping in his crib and Jenny crying on the couch that's drenched in some sort of liquid.

              GRACE
Jenny! Why aren't you at
Gran Sandy's?

              JENNY
Dale came and picked us up.
He said you wanted us back.
Mommy, I hate the smell.

Grace's gaze falls on a can of gas that's sitting in the corner.

              GRACE
Let's get out of here.

           DALE (O.S.)
You're not going anywhere.

Dale trudges into the room with a cane. He picks up the gas can and throws its content all over the floor.

> GRACE
> (to Dale) You can't stop us!

> DALE
> Am I that weak to you?!

Kyle wakes up by the bedlam and begins to whimper. Grace puts him in her arms at once.

> GRACE
> (to Kyle) It's okay.
> Mommy's here.

She looks at Dale with repulsion.

> GRACE (CONT'D)
> You're insane.

Dale holds up a lighter, smiling with a touch of cruelty.

> DALE
> Only because I can't let you go.

He flickers the lighter; a tiny flame quivers dangerously.

> GRACE
> No!

Grace sinks to her knees, Kyle still wailing in her arms. Jenny runs to her mom, scared to death.

> GRACE (CONT'D)
> Don't do it. I will stay.

> DALE

                    Can I trust you?

                         GRACE
          I promise. Please, just don't hurt my children.
                  I will do anything you want!

Tears flow down on Grace's face. Dale considers her briefly, extinguishes the fire and puts the lighter on the coffee table.
                          DALE
                 Don't hurt my feelings again.

INT. KITCHEN/GRACE AND DALE'S HOUSE - NIGHT

Grace makes a cup of tea, puts some chocolate chip cookies along with a pill on a plate.

INT. BEDROOM/GRACE AND DALE'S HOUSE - NIGHT

Delight spreads across Dale's face when Grace comes in.

                          DALE
            Cookies? What did I do to deserve you?
Grace musters up a smile.
                         GRACE
                 Your favorite. Chocolate chip.

She hands Dale the plate and sets the tea on a bedside table. Dale gulps down the dessert.

                          DALE
                     You're to die for.

Grace eyes what's left on the plate.

                         GRACE
                Oh, and don't forget your pills.

She brings the tea.

                    DALE
            Thought I've already
            finished the antibiotics.

                    GRACE
            It's for your nerves. Here.
        Grace puts the pill in Dale's palm.

                    DALE
                Thank you.
        What am I gonna do without you?

Grace raises the cup closer to Dale's lips. He pops the pill in his mouth and takes a sip of the tea. Grace smiles.

INT. BEDROOM/GRACE AND DALE'S HOUSE - NIGHT

Dale snores loudly. Grace slips out of bed.

INT. CHILDREN'S ROOM/GRACE AND DALE'S HOUSE - NIGHT

Grace wakes her daughter up.

                    GRACE
        Jenny, come on, put your clothes on.

Jenny puts on her clothes groggily. Grace stuffs some diapers and extra clothes in a bag and puts Kyle in his carrier.

                GRACE (CONT'D)
                 Let's go.

INT. LIVING ROOM/GRACE AND DALE'S HOUSE - NIGHT

Grace and the kids walk to the door as quiet as they can and as fast as they dare.

EXT. GRACE AND DALE'S HOUSE - NIGHT

They speed to Grace's car.

> JENNY
> I'm sleepy, Mommy.

> GRACE
> Shhh!

Grace hurries Jenny into the car.

INT. GRACE'S CAR - NIGHT

Grace places Kyle safely in the backseat and shoves her bag on the floor. She climbs in.

> JENNY
> Mommy!

> GRACE
> What now, Jenny!

> JENNY
> I forgot Al Capone.

> GRACE
> It's alright. Mommy will get you a new one.

> JENNY
> I want Al Capone!

Jenny is on the verge of tears. Grace sighs.

INT. LIVING ROOM/GRACE AND DALE'S HOUSE - NIGHT

Grace creeps back into the house, her eyes peeled for danger.

INT. CHILDREN'S ROOM/GRACE AND DALE'S HOUSE - NIGHT

Grace grabs a teddy bear from Jenny's bed.

INT. LIVING ROOM/GRACE AND DALE'S HOUSE - NIGHT

Grace dashes to the door and hears a click of a gun. She freezes.

>   DALE (O.S.)
>   Where are you going?

Grace, transfixed with horror, slowly turns and sees Dale's gun pointed at her head.

>   DALE (CONT'D)
>   I've been taking sleeping pills long enough to tell
>   the difference and build a
>   tolerance. You need more than one to knock me out.

Grace shudders with fear.

>   DALE (CONT'D)
>   Sit.

Dale points his cane at the couch. Grace obeys.

>   GRACE
>   I'm sorry.
>   Would you please put the gun down?

>   DALE
>   I brought that for Jenny.

Dale looks at the teddy bear in Grace's hands.

>   GRACE
>   I was overwhelmed by what happened, Dale. I don't want
>   to leave you. I never wanted --

>   DALE
>   Lie.

>   GRACE
>   You know I'll always come back to you.

Please, just listen to me.

Grace cautiously leaps to her feet.

                    DALE
             Stay where you are!

                   GRACE
          I know you love me.
   That's why you're behaving this way.
    I understand now. I really do.

                    DALE
             I said don't move!

                   GRACE
    Dale, put the gun down, please.

Dale takes a threatening step at Grace and slips on the floor that's covered in gasoline, dropping his gun. Grace runs for the door. Dale lets out a frenzied roar and seizes Grace's ankle, bringing her down.

Dale moves up to Grace's face and wraps his fingers tightly around her neck. Grace struggles wildly for her life. She gropes around and feels the cane. Grace crushes Dale's head with it and wrenches herself free as he groans in pain.

Grace sees Dale reaching for the gun. She grasps his lighter on the coffee table, lights it and throws it on him. Dale, screaming, is alight instantly. Grace grabs Jenny's Al Capone before it gets eaten by the flames.

EXT. GRACE AND HOUSE HOME - NIGHT

Grace sprints to the car.

          EIGHT-YEAR-OLD GRACE (O.S.)

> Don't leave me!

Grace turns and sees her eight-year-old self at the doorway. They look at each other.

> JENNY (O.S.)
> Mommy!!!

Grace snaps out of her mind.

INT. GRACE'S CAR - NIGHT

Grace gets in and hands Jenny her toy.

> GRACE
> Here.

EXT. GRACE AND DALE'S HOUSE - NIGHT

Grace drives, away from the house that's being swallowed up by the blazing fire.

INT. GRACE'S CAR - DAWN

Jenny and Kyle are asleep. Outside the car, the darkness lifts. Grace looks at the emerging sky, a placid smile on her face.

INT. GRACE'S CAR – LATER

Grace drives past Hazel's place and sees a "For Rent" sign.

INT. KITCHEN/JANE AND CARL'S HOUSE - DAY

Jane cradles Kyle while Grace and Jenny have a hearty breakfast.

> JANE
> I can't believe what happened.

> GRACE

I'm going down to the police station later.
They'd want to talk to me.

          JANE
What are you going to say?

Grace pulls down her collar, revealing ugly bruises around her neck. Jane gasps.

          GRACE
I'm just gonna show them this.

After a long beat.

          JANE
You're a brave girl, Grace.
You've grown up just like the way
I thought you would.

Grace puts down her fork, looking at her grandma's eggs reflectively.

          GRACE
Where's Mom?

          JANE
She left after Nancy was born.

          GRACE
Nancy?

          JANE
She gave birth to a girl a few days after
Kyle was born.

A pause.

          GRACE
Another girl, huh?

          JANE
Maybe it's her karma.

MONTAGE BEGINS INT. HOUSE - DAY

Grace cleans a house.

INT. ANOTHER HOUSE - DAY

Grace takes on painting jobs on her own.

INT. ANACONDA COMPANY - DAY

SUPER: 1974

Grace is hired by Anaconda Company. Her picture is put up on the wall with description:" First Female employed in the Trades".

EXT. HOUSE - DAY

Grace (30s), Kyle (8) and Jenny (9) move into a big, nice home which yard is fenced with trees and has a strong limb for a swing.

INT. GRACE'S HOME - CHRISTMAS EVE

Chad (16) and Charles (14) come to visit. The family has a lovely dinner together.

INT. SITTING ROOM/JANE AND CARL'S HOUSE - DAY

Grace hands Carl (80s) an envelop. He opens it and discovers a check.

CARL

GRACE
I never meant for you to pay me back.
But I want to. You don't know how
many times you and Grandma Jane have rescued me.

CARL
We don't need it.
Save it for the kids.

GRACE
I have enough to take good care of them.
You and Grandma Jane should go on a trip.
Yellowstone Park? Remember?

Carl smiles.

CARL
Of course, I do.

EXT. JANE AND CARL'S HOUSE - DUSK

SUPER: 1977

Grace and Sandy (50s) sit in front of the house under a golden sky. They are painting the big walnut tree.

For a moment, there's only the sound of their brushes stroking on the canvases.

SANDY
You're fine that Chad's
Still living with Ed?

GRACE
Yeah, I got over it. As long as Chad's happy.

SANDY
How's Ed?

GRACE
He remarried and had another son.

SANDY
You think he's still drinking?

GRACE
I'm not sure. But his new wife seems to think
she can keep him in hand just as I did.

Sandy nods understandingly.

SANDY
Kyle and Jenny like school?

GRACE
They do. I'm so happy.
But they bicker a lot at home.
It stresses me out so much.

SANDY
They are young.
You and Patty used to fight all the time too.

A smile of reminiscence passes across Grace's face.

GRACE
Me and Patty were on another level.

Sandy laughs.

SANDY
What about Charles?
He's going to the Navy.

SANDY
He is?

Grace nods.

GRACE
I'm going to sign for him.

SANDY
Of course you are.

                    You wanted to go so badly when you were his age!

                              GRACE
                 I'm glad I didn't go. I don't think I could have
                              taken the training.

                              SANDY
                          Guess Ray was right.

Grace chuckles.

                         SANDY (CONT'D)
                       Have you thought about
                  what you are gonna do now that
                       your children are older?

                              GRACE
                          Actually, I have.

                              SANDY
                             Oh, yeah?

                              GRACE
                        Remember I told you
                       I wanted to go to college?

MONTAGE BEGINS

INT. COLLEGE - DAY

Grace, with a new haircut and in a simple but elegant dress, walks down the hallway.

INT. CLASSROOM - DAY

Grace listens to the TEACHER and jots down notes.

INT. LAWN AREA/COLLEGE - DAY
Grace eats a quick lunch on the grass, leafing through a textbook.

The mellow spring wind stirs the soft fabric of her dress.

INT. LIBRARY - DAY

Grace checks out more books.

INT. CHURCH - DAY

Chad (20s) gets married. Everyone is there and wreathed in smiles. Grace watches her son with watery but joyful eyes.

INT. BEDROOM/GRACE'S HOME – NIGHT

Grace looks happily at her paper which is given an "A".

MONTAGE ENDS.

INT. COFFEE SHOP - DAY

Grace and her college friend, DANICA (20s), sit over two cups of coffee.

                DANICA
       It's nice we get to choose
      An elective course next term.
        I've always wanted to learn

                Japanese.
                 GRACE

     I don't have the muscle memory to
      learn another language anymore.

Danica laughs.
                DANICA
        What are you taking?

                GRACE
        I'm really interested in the
           creative writing class.

               DANICA
      Do you want to become a writer?

                GRACE
       I haven't given it much thought.
      But I've been reading for as long as
            I could remember.

               DANICA
        True. You live in the library.

Grace smiles.

            DANICA (CONT'D)
          Have you tried writing?

Grace shakes her head.
                GRACE
         I'm scared of picking up a
       pen and staring at a blank page.
      I don't know if I'm good enough.

               DANICA
   Grace, you're one of the most talented and
          hard-working people I know.

                GRACE
               Talented?

               DANICA
      You don't know how much you shine.

Grace casts a mediative look outside the window.

                    DANICA (CONT'D)
                    Have you been to the
                    Riverside Park?

                    GRACE
                    No.

                    DANICA
                    You should check it out
                    sometimes. It's a great place for
                    finding inspirations.

EXT. RIVERSIDE PARK – DAY

A serene place where slanting sunlight streams through the trees and multicolored flowers quiver in the bushes. Grace sits on a bench, looking languidly at the passerby.

                    GIRL (O.S.)
                    Mommy! Mommy! Look!

Grace's eyes follow the voice and fall upon a pretty girl (8) who's chasing a butterfly.

The butterfly flies away. The girl looks disappointed.

                    GIRL (CONT'D)
                    It's gone.
Her MOM (30s) walks up to her.

                    GIRL'S MOM
                    Don't worry. It will come back.

The girl tilts her head up and smiles at her mom.

                    GIRL'S MOM (CONT'D)

> Come on, let's go, my love.

Grace looks at the figures of the mother and the daughter dwindle in a distance. A smile appears on her face.
Grace takes out a notepad and a pen from her bag. She opens the pad and looks down at the page.

Grace takes a deep breath and closes her eyes. CAMERA ZOOMS IN ON HER FACE.

Grace opens her eyes. CAMERA PANS OUT.

EXT. HILLS - DAY

Grace is greeted by fresh air and endless green hills. She is on a horse under a cloudless, blue sky.

> GRACE (V.O.)
> For so long,
> I wanted to be young again and be able to
> make everything that was wrong right.

Grace looks around, a mist of tears obscuring her eyes.

> GRACE (V.O.)
> To ride bareback across the
> hills and meadow,
> to watch the lightning,
> to smell the fresh cut hay and the Northern Lights
> that brightened many winter nights.

Grace begins to ride. The horse gallops.

> GRACE (V.O.)
> I shall be forever thankful to
> those sunken memories,
> including the tears and heartache
> that once defined me.

Wind blows through Grace's hair.

                    GRACE (V.O.)
             And the laughs and joy,
               just like butterflies,
                will come back.

Grace lets out a carefree laugh, happy tears flowing freely down her face.
                    GRACE (V.O.)

              Because there is a
            beginning in everything.

                FADE TO BLACK.

THE END